Middlemost Constantine

Middlemost Constantine
Ken White

Book design by Drew Burk.
Cover design by Richard Siken.

ISBN 978-1-948510-37-0

Spork Press
Tucson, AZ
SPORKPRESS.COM

Table of Contents

1. The Hollowed Damosel

2. *The Barrow Wight*

3. *The Mercury Wall*

Middlemost Constantine

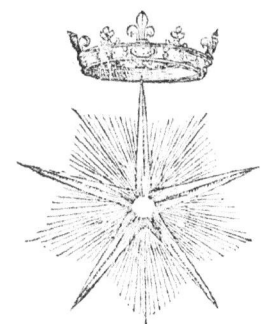

1. *The Hollowed Damosel*

infidels of my tiny afterlife
nor choice but trust
despite resistance
lightly across the crust
world slipping past
half dozen fine grade
but deepest fissures
fronted loss so terribly
who hears it through
sloping at the heel
the Lord this
between villages
tenspeed as if
I try to muster
modern veneer this
spyglass this

have pity on us no means
have pity on we who
memory carries where it will
of course feet yield the runaway
no body attached
deceits seem beyond all
though each engineers
I cannot help but laugh
this buffer bring loafers
strange fire before
after hours messenger
brandishing ramshorn
for the first time
sufficient nerve hard
goldpan this gold leaf
drowning finally

at first unholy
as long crying jag or
through diverse fibers
crenellated with
divided so much
backstage onscreen
as usual depilated
waltzes brisk quadrilles
drilled in pastures
tower hawthorn cask
I've read all versions
in iron's unruly hedge
disintegrate under fingers
attend you still rest
crumbled terraces granite
you did the stars let them

sinus pressure
amnesiac as if rising
deep water layers
scar so frequently
I thought I'd shed
waiting in the wings
Navigator delivers
misdirections we'd
with such haste glass
den of prisms marble sept
clapped unkempt
now books moth-winged
famed terminus only I
let mosses muffle all
stairs forget numbers as
be small like years

Disney voted me
history in different
for laughs check
falling all over
revises what it can't
a slight boy despite
dowsing marbles
refracted always envied
capable waist
place like this
get thee behind me
man none left but I
sentient vanguard divined
dooms conducted due
rude sextant cross
emoticon sussed

boss princess for all
corsets no take backs
my absurd lemniscate
the panoramic eye
encompass you were
abundant gifts
cowlicks the uncanny
axe handle shoulders
girl like me
irresistible thus
tender dumpling fine old
espouse you since
i.e. your convergent
diligence employed some
referenced sibylline
from morning's entrails

I pretend very well
news I don't unless
anyway that number's
who knows
my private dart
quite literally
my position
many seasons
men now outlasted
closer regard this
pool surface leaning
reflection each year's
hovers above our

I mean a thing
you catch me sneak
long defunct ask someone
someone who knows
I threw it sealed
the quick other
so well-practiced over
innumerable once young
for instance bend
cupped hand's clear
up see how in cloudless
wooden cudgel
closed old fontanels

lay me down said C-note
these our fake
most boys know betimes
they can't touch
unknown for kids like us
put on in crowds
there's no resisting
uncanny demi-victory
in the teeth of the enemy
lodged slant
little murmurs
of the eight moans
somehow

for yon silver slipper
hours we imagine
they clutches me betimes
the voice what makes yon known
that's my fun voice the one
every time I try
this current splendid
achieved at large
some flash bone
each throat nursed
for that body
and such aching
as it endured

what I loved best
convince me please with
acute acrobatics over
tribute in calibrated
I might be moved
though as if filled with
horn-nosed ravenous
remains who am I
faces of forgotten
to electrical field
the Adriatic the Adriatic
poolside inebriate at
brown young thing

served me least
something shiny
grand forum deliver
fragrances that
to marvelous clemencies
lively pupae some
runnel-boring thing
to assume various
human hindrances
stop bright recall of
a bygone span today
The Roosevelt this gleaming
rank with coconut

I want to cam with you
well past bored with
failing light socket in high wind
elephant palm defrocked
needle-of-the-sky pose
through ingress
when I breathe I forget
easily recognized by
candidly returned mirror
to my face amuses me
make-believes in
reveal secret leave-in
leaves feeling weighed
residues after only
so hard though
same poses example
pose also the pose
by steam then
in which you lean
of the needle so abruptly
all about the mirror
certain inflorescence
lies a little right
to play pretty
many dyed leathers
detangler won't leave oak
down by industrial
one lousy day of breezes

what I've done
for starters no more
book heaps still
unshelved boxed
salvage yards for themes
all else feels a bit flat less
recedes toward one form
produced ad nauseum
lead based laminates
lifeless purpled manganese
knockoff Tiffany
omissions really
since but pressing
between us heavily
honesty from exile

quick somebody kiss me
tongue than massive
unread shelved then
or better yet scoured
once desire leaves
necessary everything
among many reproductions
even faux Viennese
above the nave
until some final sun bedside
replicates host of splendid
what has time been
my mouth against the stain
transformed by hideous
all the old ills return

used to be an oxcart
its auxiliaries also
yapping Pekingese
of hand-forged
door prize at Hessian
coin purse bought
jerked it toward crafted
widths sub-umbilical
floss so promising yet
when it runs every barren
the flood now I watch
I do this manually
sundry ivories you've no
missed deliveries
at the time

was quieter than this life
neighbor's incessantly
spitted on the trident
import carving set
abbey further empty
my very own magic thumb
flagstones set in six-foot
colophon of directional
what is it about mascara
thought still ripples
for the FedEx van
as collector of perverse
idea how many
consider the kid
it seemed no thing

when Constantine perished
him I still keep a soft spot
Constantine one of twenty
precisely alike O-ringed
blameless always drowsy
collapse pledge
beside handprints
down as if life
of coals against likewise
of wright-scaled gold
despite steadfast
unyielding long

Constantine succeeded
for middlemost
creaking surcingles
with surprise and
I never sleep but entire
repeatedly dates etched
in old concrete write this
depends in any given bed
given hundredweight
lay odds on bone
efforts this perpetual
glass hour persists

was splendid brawl
than incision weather better
paroled from mildewed
by far than any
brewed up special
only nothing heals
what ever did
a scythe
this volley
most of us pretty
ownership yet I believe
tongue you wave
hand predictably

with little doctors better
than any promissory note
files of questions better
yellow headed tansy
brewed exactly the same
like it used to but
survey says
popular answer
of blank variety
confident in body
I flutter my phantom
farewell by phantom
I lift my own

going out yeah
gonna shake it what
berry berry dried
shade you detest suits
a winter I call suitors
of glamour how handy
comes in I have
some near root
so changed so many
final cigarette ground
vow draw me back
quickening toward
to despair too much after
across the centuries'
time I'm the shade

with my girls tonight
paint it up and down
blood in springtime
so well my season I'm
to my easy brand
your bag of tricks
only to touch
your distant voice
forms assumed since
against hard daylight
first moment after
sound love try not
all our situations kiss
perfect mirror only this
that orbits you

bare-assed contraposto   framed in kitchen window
dispensing entire rotisserie   chicken midnight to
three a.m. standard   devouring shift against
mighty scaffolding   of absence polished
light reminds me where   have I stashed my extra
thong whose house is this   of course in sequined
handbag was it sphagnum   moss or ringlets
that put-on by hand   your breath my actual
voice soot-streaked   dirigible scuds
unmistakable skyline   of some other reign
once thought infallible   just any one of
any morning's   endless aliases

forever sophomore diaries
me precocious minx
things the text twists it
begged when
this palsied lung
breathing it's
collusion illustrates
to find myself in
you peeled back
one simple hearth
canopy's countless
you would you knew
I wouldn't mind
of this crybaby I gag
when down to final
shut and clicked I only

everywhere malign
deceitful as with most
you commanded then
I refused as always
conniption mimics
endless still
how difficult
residence what if
this barrier kindled
beneath unblinking
pyres I wish
me well somehow
Christ get a load
on schtick truth is
charm as cleft ground
mummed the words

souped-up gastrotrucks cruise   like Hammerheads
suspended between   worlds dolled pop-up
what did new versions   become besides other
perforated versions   of themselves ever
darker asphalt varnishes   unnamed parking lot
dioramas husband take   as tithe specialty
condiments despoil   Hungarian horde
contraband ornaments   listen sweetling
without argument   I spot pure units
descending in Tetris   snowflake sequences how
infrequently when   I wish for a scissors
is there a scissors   near to hand

you me
I said it and I'm
like I do sometimes
the lamb down the well
fluttered marvelously
to make you weep
I loved your laugh
that who is there now
this sidesplitting grief
shat by the moon then
beard all night thrown
pulse the punchline
the one you think
had to walk out

I and thou there
not even kidding
that joke about drowning
wings sprouted
failed the one I told
until you laughed how
it ached so much after
in whom I might confide
it's a riot it's a doused pearl
abandoned your uncut
across my throat's
killed us you know
you were scared I
of there alone

just a couple more numb
pressure form tight seal
just give me one
too many never mind
up it doesn't matter
eye-check blue-lit
holding forth so long
me no matter what
also subject to chemicals
now than a hundred
it never blinks ask
tired to cable blah-blah
speeches blah of the great
skips ask the needle ask
solo sailors sailing

minutes keep direct
over so long since
hidden slip one extra vial
the maths don't add
everywhere bent clones
tabletops I'm done
so gone so never leaving
I'm so perplexed
something lasting less
whatevs ask geology
the gallows so too much
trick with tripped up
blah loves the record
the plagues ask so many
blazers of red sateen

lies again I lie I cleave
baddest sister as proof
of hollowed damosel
my body made
when I lay as one
your green ghost
through nude gray clutch
rabbit kits green shadow
skinned how sometime
momentarily became

I care though advertise
recall the chain
shaped weed beds
under mountain
interred with
green shoots knit
of moldering
silvers over silver hard
palest bark of you
whatever touched it

closed eyes to shell-shaped   wake where carp
mouthed the other   world then balked

taut-flanked Go-go baby
no names the way I like it no
cot at back of the invisible
person then we laugh
drops which it does whatever
in queue outside
live here all the time
planet I almost wrote
priest murder because
among dearmost loved
we don't use bodies
far too tedious
into lanes oncoming
imagine how charming
keeps me going curiosity
it it can't be long
long I really hope

off my lap for good despite
names only faded canvas
prison I confess to the invisible
like it's NYE like some jeweled ball
that means as years
gnaw velvet rope I don't
mostly I live on another
uphill sheepherder anteater
that's the language we speak
ones on my planet
all the time or even much
let us promptly veer
as a joke kind of
that last note really it's what
I still don't get can't get
now god I can't wait
that love's enough

2. The Barrow Wight

who brought sky low
raised changelings buried kings
longboats decorated inlets
pine-grained oarsmen
planted feet flag sword hips
yet helix crops long since past
contraband seeds for instance
sprouted fully formed
deployed strategic bolts
as one house against
in short if short on grief
sea ever replenishes
of other storied versions
remains a humble forge
Vulcan stooped in snow globe
trembles punishes ember
with red-orange posies
between discrete and fitful
stage hand swaps gels
this clouded lens my
broken overture next
leans hard into

stilled lake with worm and fire
offshore murdered
with ribcage installments
quickened oar-stroke
constituent roots of which
wetted with bloodlet
painted glass ingots
carved ivory pieces
flax folded twice over
never ending enemy
just wait
that's story number one
no definitive account
beneath chalk-white paling
shakes mutters frets and
battered finger pads
fresh from bellows
scenes fades igneous bouquet
and kaleidoscopic flurry fills
solitary priorate queues up
slant halt movement
each fevered minute

who else pray tell was it
to overcome wild Gaul
with stag's head torcs
sapwood stag antlered
silver rings closing
ceaseless chronicles
more common than self pay
whole of unnamed Mercia
sacrificed bound captives
"bade thee call him lord
him on knees as thy
much unrepentant giggling
stag worthy goldlike streams
fed this blackened damp
tine crowns set wide and driven
defiant temporary godheads

forsook wild Gaul
left behind cairns piled
then put to torch
bunched and bound
braid on unrecorded
note old ways
parking lots then forth rode
under sway of Danes
unabated reign
and cause thee to worship
lord" to virulent outbreak
further several nitrogen rich
into soil spattered goldlike
entablature and godlike wore
cloven stakes in sward
of laughing temporary men

unearthed in thrall to subtle wit
endeavored via diligence
endeavored all manner
gnawed spider webs to paste
yet failed to thrive
marked brow with
fluttered heaved sighed
left me by sweat and knack
such treasure as was meet
and shouldered wait
withheld robust greensticked
calcified could not resist
of course my fainting
any answers possible i.e.
long many moreover et al and
inexplicable confluence
extended more or less
breath struggle breeding
this earth like stalled baggage
enumerates ages
when kept ever under
once ungovernable now

nursed final lamed Neanderthal
without benefit of manual
concocted sustenance
ground pollen marrow watercress
husbanded breath
spit-damp kaolin
unceremoniously expired
to stow beyond all finding
an honor I bowed head
I perjure myself
femur architecturally
riddled acetabulum riddles
sickness stanched only with
what is this place how such
so forth yields same old
usual sequence variably
i.e. amniotic vomit first
birth then subsummation by mud
claim our great equalizer
in oddly drawn lots regardless
glass perishes all vast
tamed best of us

former times alas I drift
from fine bone ash
revolved on great wheeled track
reaches some oft-pillaged
but for salt and lichen
sloe-eyed lean-wristed
wrapped in cloud in
night silk gloss
a come here finger
who stole you from my orbit
keyhole storm a single
is swabbed away repeats
temporary punctuation
madness light
clutched drowning at
heart early sigils hint
stranger somehow
nerve did quicken
I set pestle to it
moan blew flame
conflagration was I then
outward robes and scepter
as briar-scabbed boy
writing selves in pooled
deciphering unerring legibles
breeze shifts standing
dawn weather a year
has not happened yet
her black hair scented peat

and sift bone fragments
court was mine great wheel
then from north most
umber shore barren
as if conjured
round-hipped
bright sheen wings
crooked like
like hey boy
pupil pressed against
bead of sweat repeats
again repeats only this
confesses hidden furnace
from shoulder shaft
tribunal this treading
offer much desired no
familiar to my sight
at nerve root
coaxed spark crushed
bade it summon
visited by final vision
that first sidereal fit
vigilant to ribbons
blood in leaves twigs
convened in cedar ribs
invitation to report
hence though the last year
thus my doom I met
and lavender and rejoiced

feather wakened ardor with
gander gray barbule pre-
its commitment read
with madness risen
after long striving I resign
walloping one side
going to launder those
abandon you denuded
caress of crocheted
mustered rows dense
inscribed alone
strong counsel admits
adjunct to this
having ransacked vocabulary
vivid epithets
scribbled sober fonts confer
officer if you please
me as you pressed
beneath graven table top
from alley underpass funny
collection hat went round
sufficient to stone properly
weight we felt we'd earned

coveted feather duster
Swiffer era as for the craft
winter madness crossbred
to eaves no new enterprise
from crude form clumped
spin cycle drum
hot buttons right off you
hostage under vigorous
cunning finger puppets
lanolin-rich calculated yarns
or in congregation
no perfunctory recourse
duty yes dread term
for invectives
fine judicious
inevitable curtain
finally won't you press
my predecessors unfortunate
heaped rubble commandeered
it was that second time
we finally gathered dregs
true other with boulevard
in our precious altogether

when she came for me
track warm ups skull
stabilize glitch moat
when she kissed she kissed
when it comes for you
there rebuke forfeit
device I inhibit with
assembles on my own
vertically to full
stark drape filleted
forest black and green
clematis choked
colonnade I walked
all sensation swung me
pendulum as day
then caved a little

she came metallic
candy headphones glitch
beneath glitch drawbridge
with chain mail lips
it will be different
some Lazarus
all breathing I insist
causeway iced
operatic height
backdrop her voice made
arcade then black
mezzanine the leafy
beneath it forswore
heelstrung as from
gave way again
more to night

neither abrogate by sweat
let deafened eyes bend
eyeglass pane as armies
levitate entire household
unrepentant nothing
invention thus reason fled
and masons in dull amaze
mutinied against calculus
herbs talismans concluded
because joint never knit
coming unborn already coupled
collective timeshare
quite clearly required
of sow warden without peer
architect of royal doctrine
instance re: details
what am I bartering
panegyric hymns my final
at thrash versus pliant
hard beneath rich raw

nor spare the red connubial
light before light raps
in uproar from afar
of the allocator
dominion of known
fastness of my boneholt
bore witness
in favor of potions
stone sank simply
now comet trumpets
to threefold death
parameters of which
that I shrug off mantle
for mucking take on
prevailed all parallel
process etc. of transmission
reason for vision
pillar forget stag
sapling forget antlers
velvet bled in tatters

panorama of inverted dead
blanket blackened
in fields of antic battle
trumpets replete with
vale in clamor
to puncture water's
venture I'd warned against
to no effect we hadn't
now alive as spinnerets
fracture crash cymbals
manic pom pom
how all humbled forces
clutter trampled grasses
gossamer some
irradiated monster
wormsoil sweetly wed
hoar-frosted red stag
relentless with gravity
egress through shambles
to branches gone scaled
taloned lateral gone sodden

clouds thick as curdle
foundry ceiling
miniature ranks
brassy spirals drown
and drowned men rise
turbid awning lost
perforce I'd warned
arms we hadn't numbers
sonic chandeliers
ganglion and ravenous
lightshow marks
in staggered heaps
then like some lost pelagic
root system dangling its
redolent of mold reeking
fungi and millipedes
whistled up a knitting needle
cleaved bulb to stem silent
I balked bolted took
furred gone feathered
with sound and madness

fervor folds me ruin
bosom rises folded it is said
culling dim projections
fashioned weeds red fescue
flapping tattered pennants
nonsense portents dull
storm blurred porthole blurs
thronged infamous host
monument of considerable
in coincidence not lost
of aggressive airline policy
now boarding gold members
dismembered children wait
crossed up with plague
air conditioned perfect
inefficient acrylic extra
economy pillow sheath

adores me ruinous
this island sinks I linger
probable inventions really
pierced upon thistles
I deduce admittedly
coordinates misapprehended
much wished for meetings with
conditionally the carnival
moment a study
on me nor dogmas
consecrated by silence
and boarding members with
wait honest mistake wires
wagons so dismiss vision
cabin pressure coddles
blanket requested over
papering this transatlantic

nine years poof
he inhabited forests ostensibly
sustained only layers of
teeming moonlit incredibles
limbic glee induced
of feral delectables
first thing awful
run that back try
next thing awful well
OK last try first thing
extemporaneous
everyone overcome
apparently evening
that's something new
missing a hand drill
workbench introduced
to the wasn't really there
a lifer he enlisted he signed
a cursive enthusiast
when they found him
for several days he refused

absconded uncounted
abandoned by chance
scrapes cuts lesions the measureless
plus sheer paroxysm
by random bonus patches
new world view deduced
next thing memory
first thing memory
it depends I suppose
memory next thing
cavity search
by awkward pauses
overstepped the mark
an entire building gone
appeared on the wrong
suddenly unfamiliar
and he listened to it
hard without flourish
enacted in triplicate
after walking so long apart
to become visible

waist to ground this velvet
bound with silk points
no shadow vestment
ordinary nightly intercourse
much degenerated from
about edges now faded
without human exit
until century raised such hymn
ends rehearsal eventual
to my purpose or leave me
of all my craft
knee-deep in granite flags
irrefutable knot wanton
ever-regenerating tendrils
swells at breath of bellows
only by tongs songs pale gold
and anvil observing all and

stallion suit of velvet black
authors iron-footed casts
only shade other
with seed cattail frond milfoil
once mighty wood alveolate
former splendor simply human
option did not occur again
long since laid by each day
disinterment so commit me
let go eternal grip
utters Vulcan long eclipsed
arc of deepened distance
green joyful sugar hydra
tangle tongues and flame-tongue
gleaming Vulcan comforted
forge coals hammer hand
for all that vision impotent

stir me now as you once convulsed
balloon whisk fingertips
some older song a simpler spell
as proprietor of astigmatisms
sundry imponderables
this world more real
of misplaced astronomies
to clip in cliffside fence
already long since stepped through
cracked glass sky
scattered cotter pins endless
by not quite snow a lighthouse
the audience never missed
scales hand-finished
canted axis long hospitable
with invitation offers framed
open-armed currents of razor

leaden pliable sky on cue
circularly countenanced
slyly murmured half uphill
conversant in
I entreat you prove
than evidence
little broken drawings
an us-sized allowance
distorted observatory curve
gridded with pilot holes
trestles inlet wracked
a dropped line or two
what with sideways grayling
by whetstone whole scheme off
unblinking sky filled
glittering embrasures
confetti to slow our fall

goad no more my nature
hold I mean reverse
drooling sanguine over
warning canticle fills me
just as all incarnations
warning no clever
the descriptive bit
visible other trifles
with wreaths laurels
portable belvedere
with tinsel crowns
grass trampled round
with many-colored ribbons
bushes tremble unto stillness
and hammered fit begin

toward wantonness
this wound unbound
engraved goblet's lip
more than all garden spoils
inherit carnation
pardon fits precisely
of no compact rendered
lauded by mill rind
light flammable
molding crowned
flowered garlands
Maypole corseted
while in coupled clusters
prove all things wrought
and end encircled

who by feats of compass
heretofore impossible
atop still impossible
beheld final trilithon
once dung-pelted
like wandered-in stock
my blue-black tongue
not yet proper words for
in crevices suckled at
shepherd boy driving
breeze-knit crook
tall and bearded bore
coat pinned closed
I rose climbed
beheld burnished towers
lamps exceeding hunter's
then transfixed and
to my end so still
consummation with
windblown incessant
elides canted louvers
ceaseless questions never
even now remain fixed
grain even now I hear it
clogging corners pounding
even now by ink I bind you
by ink I bind you

and hydraulics set
lintel stone flat
pillars leaned back
gloated a little
urchin driven off
through downed fences
swollen with languages
thirsted for them
pebbles stoop-backed
cloud of birds before with
then kettle-chested
knot bore hood torn
over shadows between ribs
great gnarled cliff oak
distant slate and silver restless
belt in countenance
held forever ransom
and ever starveling toward
affliction this weak
voice through veil and curtain
whispers coordinates
did I depart that branch
inside it spiral inside spiraled
slipping under doors
from this page's prison bars
to this our common charge
I call you from this pulp

3. The Mercury Wall

first mare's tail blinds
alluvial nerve map
terrycloth beach towel starred
shaken out debrided
interiors secretly purpling
this time properly
sufficient to endure this
rivetless vibration this
unfixed from current
endorsement first imprint
might have departed
ago how metropolitan how
normalcy swinging bar
of pieties many contaminated

me bright pang sears
into vivid matte blue
with acute granules
from all contused
post impact
embalm me with stimulant
unglamorous loose oscillating
Air King blading history
again surprise cedes
allows mint condition
several slipcovers
commanding in intimate
to bar with greatest
with exquisite sentences

so this is the world apparently
considerably stiff tariff
hitch in portside lagging
ad hoc repairs made to failing
examines hairline for
nothing astute
can't rectify focused
consigns fine-throated
predicament not unlike
of drowning scratched
classroom desks
evidently starts unguarded
to imitate resilience
litter arena in haphazard
wick catches then

so to world I surrender
vulnerable tissues snarled
leg the one cross hatched
apparatus my confessor
hairline fractures
application of airbrush
pigmented exhalation
avenues to false
historical descriptions
across undersides of
chewing gum dried hard
infant ears can't know yet
via conjured gorget so
make-believe litters until
mercury-lined lungs give in

chart this spiny acolyte
through me martial
let bleed all admittance
sundry Kool-Aid powders
just add fluids all of them
before we second guess it
corroded battery electrodes
baking soda concoction
barbed plenary born
I speak myself complicit
though find myself

meteor please spiral
velocity muster far greater
down staircase replete with
sprinkled whole sparkle mess
add them quickly
or just polish up
with Coca-Cola toothbrush
strips clean in half a jiff
plural as I was
with conspirator
alone in every room

how many times
did you beseech me never
double in the inevitable
to surfeit of direct
remain to me during long charter
to sunlight pills
the host world
interloping entity usually
shedding pale cheese-like
several tubes corresponding
for many years that despite
respectfully declines
participate in general
by mimicking footwork
for instance review
social dance subway
eviscerating robotics
actually to high five
concern more importantly
host in the left corner
weighs in some vast figure
hoists broad gold belt
ring also host crowd
as interloping stripling
but micrograms don't
ta-da! host voice swells
stripling feels every shout
and when host bell sounds
alien to established
reintroduced to

times irredeemable
make do with only one
event that I succumb
sunlight what stratagems
cruise without recourse
in tall dark bottles
does not reject immediately
small form red-patched
substance squalling and attached
encumbrances may not recognize
best effort host world
all resultant patterns
melee largely governed
facial expressions expected
rituals correct fork usage
flirting the exquisitely
of small talk when
without drawing undue
when to stop however
rich black trunks
with undetermined exponent
jigs from side to side at center
loses collective host mind
in gray gauze weighs in
register on the scale
deafens with tumult
and hiss as stripe of host whip
knows will again be found
everything and summarily
outermost orbit

I forget nothing
triple it and still
all braids evenly divided
each trail I know
world being as world has become
Celsius charts
conspiratorial bridge
an afterlife of sorts
dissertations in after hour
of tumblers each thick
I aggregate and emit
3D printer I inhabit
among hour-counters
into ill-fitting trousers
with solitude
in season one
on which entire constituency
and diagrammed fit
two the plot is lost

think of a curse
you're nowhere near
from earth
leads downhill eventually
parts per million
red-oranging out at top etc.
between parched environs
kind of thing studied
archives behind system
as all minerals
as if sprung from forehead of this
not an uncommon concern
cramming the fitting scheme
wind-felled wire-crossed encounter
the mouth that devours
time is a flat disc
served up trussed and horned
for partition in season
the map does not exist

swabbed my mind
doused cavity with isopropyl
tinactin what was handy
I applied without restraint
in any case endless scroll of
diplomacy feed never
each subsequent summer
of which my linen subdues
vessels ambrosial
pier-to-pier at 1000x interior
organelles organized
don't repeat this like you
pry open this sleeping company
the deepest key lost at the
reverie so often attributed
living hard and upright
hazarding some greater dark
of long division
paraffin gel bleach tough actin
from the cabinet
not my strongest point
followers clicks my false
ends conscripts me into
wedding the underarms
with dark half-moon
phosphate surfactants
replicates on the slide
in crested vessels christ
promised last and failed
pressed and sealed
she parted it is said
to everything served up
as tilted corner oar
against brightening window scar

for poker face let play
unsealed envelope leopards
former tumbler conditions
cue moving foliage off screen
cardigans of past versions I deleted
there was a cunning word
to which I promised my lasting
nuzzled nurtured and swore
once known doors the tradeoff
don't worry about it I said
spools of tacit winding
style how every era
possibility when I go
up and down me reminisce
stilled in mud rendered me
so display case

this blank menagerie
swallowed known
of duplicate house key
lank-limbed clever fellows slouched
sent flowers the hard way wait
from last night's book
devotion repeated out loud
to remember but new rooms close
keeps coming for me
I'm buried already
sheet in passing fair
could fossil such rigid
prop me in the corner type it
how once tiny boney fish
thus so whole so revealed
naked entire

yours in torchlight
note how few genuine distractions
a lot of dancelike gestures
wisdom a noise producer once
cotton batting essentially
impersonating scallops
evinced by interior decorator
make out word one
inevitable confection
for that thing
folded into imposter
fox clutching effigy
with filched egg in jaws
origin a long abandoned
embossed at seam where
dungeons full of plastic
mirror smooth surface
untroubled by its own
despite actual eons of

we audit our equipment
present as distraction first
cleansed of label
related through epic
endless strips of lemon squares
also a nice gesture
all in all couldn't
but nodded prolifically agreed
plus headache powder
I can't remember
no a poster of an origami
of fox proper
blue roan speckled Fabergé
Pyrenees castle permanently
post mortem revealed
cherry blossoms asphyxiating
apparently bottomless moat
vouchsafed harmless dark
evidence to the contrary

finally time let the curses out
let mummified mice
found on of a set of earrings
according to astral charts
provenance extraterrestrial
from every multi-celled something
human membranes in fact
abstracted into consciousness
inescapable bias
guard vile cherub
little messed up rose-cheeked
waiting room crowded with
cards and balloons
from sky just like you did and

drained casks of dust and lime
plunder mummified grain
prehistoric indescribable
of common matter deduced
hue and cry lifting
contained in variably expandable
thing itself becomes
via sheer thick concavity
what I'm losing forward
of marching decrepitude
lamb-kitty nauseating
relatives and flowers
of course unidentifiable metal fell
not even that long ago

humps of huddled malcontents
rusted axle from a half-ton
of flowers I don't know
no list of local species
I would starve for want
fail to report how
far off corrugated tin roof
shone devoutly and so forth how
for little torn dolly
Ann or Andy barefoot
I also tra-lee tra-lah found
pine needles and

in pinwheel formation
something the names
them also I own
varieties of house spiders also
of ready tubers would further
sun smote with ragged nail file
just so and tra-lee tra-lah oh how
being lost in the wood I wept
raggedy little handmade gingham
the memory of bottle shard
buried in copper
not by glint

insouciant sonic jellyfish drift
blue coronet lit
membrane outside my skin
breath marks how
I'll find you on the floor
drained in the blushing tub
considerably lighter once
I don't know what hides
correction
I've mapped on charts
labeled and deduced
correction
redacts its joke relents
time continuously redeploys
to the dead in a tongue
hint it sounds
hint can't not do it
and stop them
I've gotten so much older so
likewise fail me a failure
like home is hard
or now I mean
a thing suspected
form arranges approximation
I hear congratulations
your save the date where
are you due it's a girl
complaining I'd imagined
life before all these
how it's done the being
over tracks I've run this
above blue-lit stove
despite emollient industrial foam
so delicate that any errant
one certain-making day
or you will discover me
or tipped back in passenger's seat
the hardest part has flown
in me to make me feel this
accumulated irreducibles
graphs measured parsed
clog all reason
time takes minute refuge
again not quite it's just that
how we speak
they might comprehend
exactly the same
and no need just try
they speak to me
very quickly and skyscrapers
I reciprocate hard
I don't mean here
the place I've never been
can't uncleave while this
fine weather's a blessing
are in order received
are you registered when
it's a boy it's a ruse stop
some better no different
promises I don't know
here repeatedly running
variation played out

letters pressed with
into note pad then
my cheek undersheet
perceived understood perfectly
there's no place I keep
I promise you but

lead-breaking intent
detective held against
indelible with compressions
legible then forgotten
telling you like it
I've never been there

you who once gilded me
aerosols inked me ballpoint
inks of which
icy and minute
sinks below oozing
confederate wreaking
fingers its
so near completion
boiling surface curves
failed utterance I cannot
said usage of the imaginary
permeable-at-last wall
alone no ignored no
known but

with glittering
fine these exalted
a darkling dispensation
barbarous of bathroom
medicine cabinets my coy
by slippery
considerable havoc
this impersonation project
away beneath site of first
condone in myself
brittle sonorous
prefer to be left
I prefer not to be
omitted

quorum for solo
yields quotient exceeded yes
harbor in my sweater so
and people annoy me surely
at least imagine
to let rope slip
into mist and wouldn't
relief to embrace or
from across the room
prohibitively goofy faces
my face is changing into three
one dwarf star I'm not
or doing right by
turn it down back it
as a silent movie
there are four stags
stacked on top
foxes horses greyhounds
I subtract from the tale
I lift my chin
to rest it in

performed in tandem
meal was delicious its molecules
thanks people I am people
one empathizes or can
what I want
and skiff ease
that come as considerable
at least to flirt with
via entire repertoire of
that's not a bruise
earth-like planets orbiting
doing earth right
earth I keep saying
off shoot the entire scene
on this card
there are two boars
of two boars more ditto
and the row
the whole reason
to camera and pretend
the image of your hands

allow me just this minute
staring into middle
the force with which
tore all hinges off
collapsed as time does
through tangled conduit
every last thermometer
every other second confirms
moored and unmoored
that held escape
has not checked in curbside
watching paper lamps float off
mountain range and blowing
split decision you
for me and time
do eventually just before
though now listen

or minute and a half
distance I can't believe
the door that wasn't there
the wall then wall
perpetually when I'm poured
like Silver Surfer broke and drank
uncharacteristic zoom in
world still simultaneously
the fastening pin
balloon to ground
I'm waiting at the gate
across some twilit
on my hand where you engraved
remembered me
collapsed again all walls
untearable metal tears
how the clock rubs thin

wise kind god of minor treacheries
shared aisles cubicles
consider some universal cure
flatscreen made heavy luminous
turns out been trained up
maximal wisdoms first
followed by the double trick
say eleven seconds ago
in retrospect I'd trade it all
redundant though
to comprehend you in cycles
cancellous then cold then
note by note
scattered wands of you
what I swallowed for
you now inhabit me despite
charms tidal contrivances
your gatling lungs
indecipherable wise blind
by my knobs my dials
disguised as tender you will
uncountable freckled assemblages
over basin's dromedary hump
arranged avowed pledged
pact long crushed
you've kept me pressed
endless files again

think how synchronous
these broad fluorescent eyes
backlit incident room
under sufficient scrutiny
on the sly received seven
and foremost scalding by rote
of several hours since
and the year into which
to have been made
by happenstance I've come
skin muscle gristle wondrous
infinitesimal subtraction
strand by strand
yet sleep the winter out
the lesson of you I admit
static interference vaccines
though forced to tongue
by repetition made
god of nothing special know me
my wires and coarse devices
know me by contests lost
disposable razor improvises
though indentured though
somehow forsworn though
though years on years
between pages of your
I open to you and rust

big talk bold talk
I was lost
even the most stalwart
into sixes and sevens
unsettled vengeful vexed
from center of my best
beneath adhesive flap
then lost in mail
woolen tongue
on coat tree or name
itself cast casually
tufted back or crumpled
where your buttoned edge
as they must have always
I never pray but please
surely I'm not only over
that die all blow away
a shield a cyclic mutiny
once more above this
we keep returning
who sent us here
of question as one might
fluid through a maze
of crumbled sepulchers
proposition stricken
free fall feels like
submersion or

once snow softened
all softened failed fled
thirteens can be broken
as I can a little
admittedly derailed somewhat
waxed and sealed
long since licked
say again says this same
in coat check or hooked
another impromptu rack
over threadbare couch's
on some other chair
elides my raveled hem
so do not disappear again
do not disintegrate
and over the parts of me
before the sudden door
a warning beacon lit
illuminated reef to which
immune to years the answer to
instead commit pursuit
to some chance messenger
of worn names a village
this whole existence
with ellipses though
spiral an eruption
beginning

Acknowledgements

I'm especially grateful to Marie-Helene Bertino, Brian Blanchfield, Drew Burk, James Meetze, Danielle Pafunda, and Richard Siken for their generosity, insight, inspiration, and support as this book took shape.

I'd also like to thank the editors of *BOMB Magazine*, *Bright Bones: An Anthology of Contemporary American Writing*, *EuropeNow Journal*, *Horsethief*, *Omniverse*, and *Talking River*.

The illustrations are taken from Claude Paradin's *Devises Heroïques* (1557).

KEN WHITE is a poet and screenwriter. He co-wrote and co-produced the feature film *Winter in the Blood*, co-directed and co-wrote the short film *Universal VIP*, as well as directed and co-wrote the short film *The Conservationist*, currently in development as a feature. White is the author of three books of poetry: *Eidolon*, *The Getty Fiend*, and *Middlemost Constantine*. His work has appeared in *The Boston Review*, *Columbia: A Journal of Literature and Art*, *Omniverse*, *Manor House Quarterly*, *Versal*, *Spork*, *Horsethief*, *EuropeNow*, *Poets.org*, and *BOMB Magazine*, among others. White is an Assistant Professor of Screenwriting at the University of Nebraska at Omaha Writer's Workshop, and teaches at the low-residency MFA at the Institute of American Indian Arts in Santa Fe.

CPSIA information can be obtained
at www.ICGtesting.com
Printed in the USA
FSHW021110140620
71169FS